TRACTION ENGINES IN FOCUS

by John Crawley

PUBLISHED BY
JOHN CRAWLEY LTD, TURVEY, BEDFORDSHIRE

First published in 1982 by
John Crawley Limited
Field House, Turvey
Bedfordshire MK43 8DU

Printed in Great Britain by
A.B. Printers Limited, Leicester

ISBN 0 9508046 0 6

Reprinted 1984

PREFACE

The interest in the steam engine continues to grow unabated. Each year fresh engines appear, either from enforced hibernation whilst lengthy and costly repairs have been effected, or by the sheer effort of going overseas and repatriating some rare make or type of machine that will eventually appear, as new, on one of our rally fields, beautifully painted and lined out with all the bare metal parts highly polished and glinting in the sunlight.

Many of the young and even not so young enthusiasts could be excused for thinking that in days gone by all engines appeared like this, creating a colourful addition to the streets and countryside alike.

In reality very few engines were given the standard of painting and lining out we see today. There were exceptions of course; engines built to exhibit on the makers' stands at agricultural shows were given such treatment, showmans engines were more often than not highly finished and fitted out with brass ornamentation, but there were the exceptions. Most were neatly painted with relatively simple lining out and perhaps a rather ornate transfer proclaiming to all and sundry the many awards for quality and excellence of workmanship that had been awarded to them at exhibitions long since past.

It must be remembered that today we regard engines with affection, but in the days we are discussing they were machines supplied to do a specific job, and however smart they may have looked when new within a short time they were considerably toned down by the very nature of their work.

As the years went by an oily rag or drop of paraffin was the most they could expect to receive and many were left to accumulate layers of oil and dirt which, by a curious quirk of fate, was to stand them in good stead when the day came that they were no longer required and just left standing where they were last used.

This accidental cocooning helped many of them to survive the between years when an engine was unworked — until the coming of the fifties when the preservation movement got underway.

In this album of photographs it is the intention to show engines as they really were when earning their owner's bread and butter and to present them in as large a format as possible within the confines of the chosen page size.

No claims are made that the pictures are all published for the first time, in fact quite a few have been used before in other publications, such as club magazines not generally available to the enthusiast of today, or else in expensive volumes where they have been reproduced in such a small size to illustrate the variety of a firm's products that it has been impossible to study any details of the engine concerned.

The photographs of the four Fowler Super Lion Showmans engines have been seen before, but never to my knowledge all side by side so that the many variations in fittings could be compared.

I am a firm believer that every photograph caption should give the basic details of each engine depicted, with registration numbers where known, as this all helps in identification of other photographs which might otherwise remain unidentified. The only problem that this presents is in the stereotyped captions that result.

With regard to the registration numbers given it must be realized that these were usually issued after the road traffic act of 1921; it is not uncommon to find an engine built around 1910 receiving its registration number in the mid 1920s. This would come about when the engine changed hands or the original owner wished to use it on the highway.

Where the date of building is given the month does of course signify the month of completion and the new student of traction engine history should not be misled into thinking it was built during that month, the opposite being the case, sometimes many months being taken to erect and test a new engine.

The quality of photographs is very dependent on the clarity of the original and rather than omit a very old and interesting picture it has been included and the printers have made every effort to get the best possible results.

I sincerely hope that the perusal of the photographs in this album will provide you with many happy hours of study, the older enthusiast re-living the past and the younger getting an insight to how engines really looked when they had to work for their living.

This album began to be compiled many years ago but regretfully it had to be shelved until recently, with the sad result that many of my friends have passed on. However I must thank all of those who have so generously assisted me, either with the loan of old photographs or else with the identification of many of the older prints.

My thanks therefore go to: R. Addis; D. Burnage; British Rail (Eastern Region); M. Carroll; W.B Chambers; K. Dickens, A.V. Evans late of Fodens Ltd; A. Fensom; G. Fensom; The Henry Ford Museum; A. Ibbot; Major H. Marshall; E.A. Olive late of Aveling Barford; R.G. Pratt; C. Roads, A.E. Smallbone of Wallis & Steevens; J. Smith; R. West and the late F.H. Gillford, S. Harrison, J. Mellor, C. Quick and T.B. Paisley.

Finally, I would particularly like to thank Alan Duke for enduring my continual queries on details of ownership and to David Phillips of the Museum of English Rural Life at Reading who assisted in the identification of so many of the old works photographs in my collection.

These two works photographs are of 5nhp single cylinder traction engine No 3344. Built November 1911 and sold to the Limerick County Council as their fleet No 5. The photograph above shows the engine standing across Minstergate Street with the Burrell offices forming the background. The photograph below has the background painted out. Note the engine has been photographed without the motion cover side plates in position.

Wallis & Steevens 5nhp single cylinder traction engine No 2381, Registration No HO 6044. Built August 1896 and sold to J. Stevens of Upottery, Devon. She was returned to the works within a year. In 1897 she was sold to J. Rankin of Limavady in County Londonderry, again within a year she was returned to the works. In 1898 she was sold to W. Northgate of Arlesford, Hampshire who purchased the parts to convert her into a roller in 1899.

Wallis & Steevens 5nhp single cylinder traction engine No 2505, Registration No OH 5651, built April 1902 and sold to G. Hickson of Wellow Gate Works, Grimsby.

ЛcLaren 7nhp single cylinder :raction engine No 616, ?egistration No HD 1493, built 'uly 1898 and supplied to Hampshire Bros of ?avensthorpe, Nr Wakefield n Yorkshire. This engine was one of four that was sent back nto the works for a repaint and the fitting of a special wire rope. She then toured all over the country letting up a captive balloon advertising *Hudsons Soap*. Their name was affixed to a special plate on the valve chest over and on a bracket over the coal bunker.

ЛcLaren 8nhp single cylinder :raction engine No 688, built 'anuary 1901 and supplied to George Glover of Darrington n West Yorkshire. She was eventually purchased by A. Clarke of Kirksmeaton. This picture shows her at work baling straw near Pontefract n July 1946.

ЛcLaren 6nhp single cylinder :raction engine No 660, ?egistration No HD 1492, built March 1899 for George Hampshire of Batley, Yorkshire. This threshing scene was photographed at Staincliffe Hall Farm near Dewsbury in August 1935, the driver Jim Smith first drove this engine at the age of fourteen.

Ransomes, Sims and Head 6nhp single cylinder traction engine No 5137, built April 1882 and exhibited on their stand at the Newmarket agricultural show that year. She was sold in August to an Irish agent by the name of Collins of Drogheda for his customer L. McKeown also of Drogheda. She then spent the next 79 years at work until she was seen in the grounds of the Salesian Agricultural College in County Meath. The magazine *The Engineer* in their edition of the 6th December 1878 gave a review of this class of engine and stated, 'Many of these engines are at work and giving great satisfaction and we understand that farmers find that in their present perfect state it is much more economical to use them for hauling about their threshing machines, than to employ horses for drawing the portable engine and threshing machine from farm to farm'.
This engine is now back in England, fully restored and still capable of doing a day's work when called upon. These photographs were taken at the Agricultural College in 1961.

Burrell 7nhp single crank compound traction engine No 2597, Registration No NO 3949, built July 1903 and sold to A. Coulson of Milton, Cambridgeshire. In this photograph she is seen whilst with her recorded owner, John Patten of Little Hadham and it would seem she was cut up for scrap sometime after 1952.

Wallis & Steevens 8nhp single cylinder traction engine No 2059, Registration No BH 8737, built August 1886 and sold to Pritchard & Woodley of Burnham, Buckinghamshire. She had only this one owner and by 1945 she had been sold for scrap.

Burrell 6nhp single crank compound traction engine No 2143, Registration No NM 139, built November 1898, she was sold to J.W. Ridgeway of Skimpot, Bedfordshire. In this picture she is seen on the 19th September 1936 when with her new owners R.W. Howling & Sons of Ingoldisthorpe, Norfolk. the previous day she had been delivered from dealers George Thurlow of Stowmarket in black livery. Her new owners had painted her green overnight.

Burrell 7nhp single crank compound traction engine No 2520, Registration No CE 8015, built October 1902. Seen here in the ownership of J. Nicholls & Sons of Cheveley, Cambridgeshire on the 10th April 1939.

Wallis & Steevens 8nhp single cylinder traction engine No 2383, built April 1898 and sold to E. Loader & Sons of Sherbourne St Johns, Hampshire.

Wallis & Steevens 7nhp single cylinder traction engine No 2842, Registration No HO 5962, built September 1906 and sold to A.A. Varby of East Boldre, Hampshire. She appears to have spent the whole of her working life with this owner.

Fowell 7nhp single cylinder traction engine No 84, Registration No NN 3506, built circa 1898 and sold to W.J. Bird of Farnsfield, Nottinghamshire. She changed owners twice before being bought in 1947 by the Lincolnshire firm of Butler & Green. She spent the rest of her working life with them until cut up in 1962.

Ransomes, Sims and Jefferies 6nhp single cylinder traction engine No 26978, Registration No CT 4221, supplied to the Ministry of Munitions in November 1916. By 1921 she was in the ownership of G.H. Chamberlain of Billinghay, Lincolnshire, who last licensed her in 1947. This picture shows her on war work at Kenilworth, Warwickshire in 1917.

Marshall 6nhp single cylinder traction engine No 79128, Registration No CT 8288, built April 1925 and exhibited on Marshall's stand at the Dublin Show in that year. Later she was sold to John Croft of Naburn in the East Riding of Yorkshire. In this photograph she is seen threshing at Riccal, Yorkshire in 1935.

A photograph taken by Burrells in their works yard showing an inner firebox with a collapsed crown. Unfortunately the cause of the failure is not recorded. The details of the firebox can be clearly seen; the bridge stays supporting the top of the box, the foundation ring which shows the width of the water space between the inner and outer boxes, and the stays which have all been cut to allow the box to be removed from the engine.

Wallis & Steevens 8nhp single cylinder traction engine No 2458, built 1899 for Whitaker Wright of Godalming, Surrey. Later in her life she was bought by W.A. Gillson of Middleton, near Market Harborough.

Wallis & Steevens 7nhp single cylinder traction engine No 2842 Registration No HO 5962, built 1906 and sold to A.A. Vardy of East Boldre, Hampshire.

Marshall 6nhp single cylinder traction engine No 29944, Registration No AL 9271. Built in July 1898, she was sold at the Lincoln Show in that year to Joseph Fox of Sibthorpe, Nottinghamshire. By 1943 she was in the ownership of R.A. Hough of Bathley, and in this picture taken in 1946 at Coddington, nr Newark, she is setting off with a threshing drum and elevator in tow.

Ruston Proctor, 7nhp single cylinder traction engine No 13803, built December 1888 and delivered to J.A. Cole of Roxholme Hall, Sleaford, Lincolnshire. This photograph was taken at Denby in 1924.

Fowler 6nhp compound class A7 road locomotive No 13091, Registration No MA 8622, built October 1913 for W.A.R. Hoare of Bovey Tracey, Devon. After a number of different owners it was purchased by Morley Bros of Castleford, Yorkshire and converted to a showmans engine named *Our Lizzie.* Sometime in 1947 it was bought by H. Steel of Ardsley, nr Wakefield. This photograph of a typical scene shows her threshing near Wombwell on the 3rd April 1952.

Marshall 7nhp single cylinder traction engine No 54587, Registration No AJ 5781. Built July 1910 and sold to Edward Holliday of Topcliffe at the Yorkshire Show that year. She later passed to M&N Alderson of Stavely. In this view she is seen hard at work in April 1957.

McLaren 8nhp single cylinder traction engine No 452, Registration No CF 3821, photographed on the 16th March 1938 in the ownership of A. Baldock of Haverhill, Suffolk. Note the deflector on top of the chimney to help with raising steam and the poker leaning against the rear wheel.

Two views of a magnificent Burrell 12nhp single cylinder straw burning traction engine No 3053. Built November 1908 for sale to a customer in Buenos Aires, South America. The special ashpan, water filled spark arresting chimney top and ramp for dragging up the straw bales for feeding into the firebox are all points worthy of note.

A Cooper traction engine with double high pressure cylinders and horizontal shaft steering takes part in the Coronation celebrations of King George V in the summer of 1911. The engine with three wagon loads of children anxious parents walking and a drum and bugle band bringing up the rear is seen leaving the village of Broughton, Northamptonshire en route for a picnic.

Wallis & Steevens 8nhp 'T' class single cylinder traction engine No 253 *Industry*, built 1878 and sold to T. Hibberd & Son of Basingstoke.

Fowler single cylinder class O straw burning traction engine No 10345, built October 1905. Between the years 1905 and 1909 Fowlers built fourteen of these Anglo-Argentine engines as they were called, all were ordered by a Luis Gely and presumably all were sent to the Argentine.

A fine photograph of a Burrell single crank compound traction engine *Earl of Devon*, owned by Henry Arden of Heavitree, Exeter seen at work driving a rack saw bench. Unfortunately no further details are known about this engine.

Aveling & Porter 8nhp single cylinder traction engine No 1946, Registration No AP 9327, built March 1884 and sold to J. & H. George of Woodchurch, Kent. By August of the following year she had changed owners and was with J.H. Vane of High Halden, Kent. By 1921 she had moved again this time to Rye in Sussex, where she is seen in this photograph threshing whilst in the ownership of Reeves & Selmes.

Hornsby 8nhp single cylinder portable engine of 1876, photographed at Orston, Nottinghamshire in 1916. Note the wooden wheels.

Allchin 6nhp compound traction engine No 1529, Registration No, KE 2725. The Allchin records for this period are missing so that the date of building and the original owners are not known. By 1921 she belonged to the Wingham Engineering Co Ltd in Kent, who used her until they advertised her for sale in 1948. This photograph shows her at work at Cranbrook, Kent in 1920.

Wallis & Steevens 6nhp single cylinder traction engine No 2233, Registration No HO 5817. Built in July 1893 for J. Dewe, Hampstead Norris, Berkshire, she was supplied with the tank wagon seen in the photograph. On the rear of the engine's tender was mounted a rotary pump for filling the tank, this was belt driven from the flywheel.

Fowler 7nhp compound road locomotive Class R, No 8435, Registration No NM 5046, built December 1899 and delivered to Mutter Howey & Co of Newcastle-upon-Tyne. She eventually changed owners before being bought by George Taylor of Redbourn, Hertfordshire. The well known engine dealer who sold her in 1924 to Ralph Savage of Riseley, Bedfordshire, who named her *Thora* and used her in his threshing business.

Wallis & Steevens 15 ton single cylinder steam roller No 2255, Registration No KE 9507. Built August 1892 and sold to the Gillingham Local Board (later Gillingham Borough Council). She spent all her working life at Gillingham until sold for scrap to R. Wanstall & Son of Rainham, Kent in 1948.

Wallis & Steevens 6 ton single cylinder steam roller No 2817, built 1905, sold to the Crown Agents and exported to Singapore. Specially fitted pulley on extended crankshaft and supplementary fuel bunker mounted on tender side for local fuel.

Aveling & Porter 6nhp compound 6 ton steam roller No 11670, Registration No SN 3875, built November 1926 and sold to Dunbartonshire County Council. Later on she was bought by H. Richards & Co Ltd, of Newport, Monmouthshire and became their fleet No 21. Sold in 1959 to Potter Bros of East Dereham, Norfolk.

These two steam rollers were en-route from H. Richards & Co Ltd, of Newport, Mon., to Potter Bros of Dereham in Norfolk in March 1959. The train was seen passing through Woburn Sands station and both rollers were seen to be in good order. At Bedford they were taken out of the train and shunted into a siding for inspection as No 12181 had by now suffered a broken front fork. *(see left)*. As many goods trains used to stop and pick up loaded wagons at the brick works it is possible that some rather heavy shunting was the cause.

Aveling & Porter 6nhp compound 6 ton steam roller No 12181, Registration No DW 6156, built July 1928 for H. Richards & Co Ltd, of Newport, Monmouthshire. Sold to Potter Bros of East Dereham, Norfolk.

Burrell 8 ton convertible compound steam roller No 3839, Registration No AH 0750, built July 1920 and sold to Johnston Bros of Horsehay, Salop. By 1921 she had changed owners and belonged to the Staffordshire Haulage & Contracting Co Ltd of Wolverhampton.

Burrell 10 ton compound steam roller No 3943, built April 1923 and fitted with an Allen scarifier. Supplied to a customer in South Africa.

Burrell 8 ton compound steam roller No 4062, Registration No YB 9360, built April 1927 and sold to W.J. King of Bishops Lydeard, Somerset, who retained her in their business until 1970.

Aveling & Porter 5 ton compound tractor No 11385, Registration No KM 1216, built December 1925, for the Kent County Council, their fleet No 27. By 1937 she belonged to John Allen & Sons of Cowley, Oxford, who converted her into a roller of dubious charm. In this picture she is seen at work in Bedford in May 1939.

Aveling & Porter convertible compound steam roller No 5822, Registration No F 1619, built September 1905 for B.W. Glenny of Romford, Essex. By 1921 she belonged to H.G. Rose of Beccles and carried the Registration No AH 0567. This picture shows her in the ownership of Edward J. Edwards of Norwich, rolling a private road at Much Beggars Hall, Claydon, Suffolk in April 1935.

Robey 7 ton tri-tandem compound steam roller No 43755, Registration No VL 1412. This engine was built in June 1929 as a tandem roller and delivered new to Wirksworth Quarries Ltd, Derbyshire. She was one of three that they converted by adding an extra rear roll. In this view she is seen at Ridgmont, Bedfordshire rolling the top dressing on the M1 Motorway shortly before its opening.

This photograph was taken at Grimsby in 1932. At that time a well known firm by the name of 'Bannisters' were importing some patent road making substance called *Kyrock* which looked like soot and was imported from the continent in bags. Messrs Bannisters got the Borough Surveyor interested in this material, the surveyor at that time, a Mr Wyatt, being a friend of the Managing Director of Marshall, Sons & Co Ltd who agreed to loan the 4 ton tandem roller to roll it for him. Queen Street was selected as this short length was considered to have more traffic over it than any other in Grimsby.

Fowler 10 ton single cylinder Class DH steam roller No 14672, Registration No HO 6087. Built in July 1922 and sold to E.W. Wright of Alton, Hampshire, she is seen posing for her official works photograph. Note the non-standard chimney top.

Fowler 15 ton single cylinder steam roller Class A4 No 7631, built March 1897 for Minett & Jackson of Woodlesford, Yorkshire. Could the two important looking gentlemen in the horse and trap possibly be Mr Minett and Mr Jackson checking up on the men at work and no doubt eager to be included in the photograph?

Aveling & Porter 15 ton single cylinder steam roller No 1565, Registration No BC 4774, built January 1880 and supplied to Leicester Corporation, their fleet No 1. This roller is fitted with the early type conical front rolls utilising a centre pivot. They proved very unsatisfactory in use as they tended to skid rather than roll. Cotton reel type steering was also fitted.

Aveling & Porter 6 ton compound tandem roller No 7152, Registration No AU 4979, built August 1910 and sold to the Nottingham Corporation. This type of roller was notorious for slipping sideways on cambered roads whilst proceeding forwards. This photograph was taken in Nottingham in 1916.

Aveling & Porter 10 ton single cylinder steam roller No 2507, Registration No BE 7722, built June 1889 for York Corporation, their fleet No 2. She received the Registration No CT 5197 when owned by Arthur M Cole of Roxholme, Lincolnshire.
This photograph was taken at Arnold, Nottinghamshire in 1926 by which time she was owned by F.H. Gillford.

A most interesting works photograph of a Burrell single crank compound steam roller. The eccentric driven pump, the gear change mechanism, and the crankshaft and valve gear layout can be plainly seen as can the numerous oiling points which will require the frequent attention of the driver.

Fowler 12½ ton single cylinder Class D2 steam roller No 7499, Registration No NL 8297, built December 1895 and supplied to John Foggo & Son of Choppington, Northumberland and delivered by rail to Morpeth station. In this photograph she is fitted with Eddison & De Mattos Patent Henderson Road Scarifier which has rotating drills driven by a belt from the flywheel.

Another view of the same class of steam roller illustrated above but showing the flywheel side. This is No 7646, built October 1896 and sold abroad. Extras include governers and the luxury of a seat.

Aveling & Porter 10 ton single cylinder Class AD steam roller No 14147, Registration No YD 4740, built April 1932 for Weston-Super-Mare Urban District Council. In 1949 she was acquired by W.W. Buncombe of Highbridge, Somerset and became their fleet No 150. This photograph shows her at work at Hadleigh in Suffolk.

A delightful works photograph of a Wallis & Steevens steam roller scarifying a road in Basingstoke. No other details are known.

Burrell 10 ton compound steam roller No 3313 *Scout*, Registration No AH 6813, built August 1911 for Doran Bros, of Thetford, Norfolk. She worked for this well known firm of rolling contractors until *circa* 1960 when she was purchased by R. Palmer & Sons of West Dereham.

Fowler long firebox Class D2 compound steam roller No 11095 *Conqueror*, built February 1908 for George Eastwood of Emley, Yorkshire. She was last reported in the ownership of William Tawse Ltd, of Aberdeen.

Fowler Class T1 compound steam roller No 12522, built February 1912 and exported to Bombay, India.

Aveling & Porter 10 ton single cylinder steam roller No 4907, Registration No FX 6929, built November 1901 for the Eddison Steam Rolling Co Ltd of Dorchester, their fleet No 98. The foreman resplendent in a bowler hat poses his men for the photographer. It is interesting to note that the drive shaft to the pump along with the pump plunger have been removed.

Robey 7 ton tandem compound steam roller No 42523, Registration No FE 7855 which was new for the Public Works and Road Transport Exhibition in November 1925, Limmer & Trinidad Lake Asphalt Company Ltd took delivery on the 6th March 1926. In this view she is seen working at Ranelagh Road, Ipswich.

Robey 6 ton tandem steam roller No 43394, Registration No YW 8199, built June 1928 and supplied to the Metropolitan Borough of Stepney. A number of interesting features may be seen in this photograph; the pistol type boiler and firebox, chain drive and the flywheel mounted on the offside end of the crankshaft.

Robey 12 ton 'Lion' type steam roller believed to be No 43693, Registration No VL 174, built April 1928 and sold to Tilbury Contracting & Dredging Co Ltd.

Fowler 8nhp Class B1 compound road locomotive No 5749, built May 1889 for J.D. Robinson of Bridgehouse, Sheffield and McLaren 8nhp road locomotive No 132, built October 1881 for John Whittaker of Edenfield, Lancashire. This photograph taken in 1899 shows them both in the ownership of W. Carter of Manchester, whilst taking a 40 ton boiler from Robert Taylor and Sons of Marsden to Bury in Lancashire, a total weight of 55 tons behind the engines.

Fowler 8nhp Class B5 compound road locomotive No 8473 *Jesmond*, Registration No NL 1599. Built September 1900 for William Bland of Gosport, Northumberland. This photograph taken *circa* 1920 shows her with a load at Newcastle Quay.

Two of Allen Knights McLaren road engines about to set off on a long journey in June 1916. The leading machine is 10nhp compound No 775 *The Conqueror*, Registration No WR 6663, built January 1905 for Reynolds and Haselgrave of Wakefield. The following engine is 10nhp compound No 776 *Yorkshire Bob*, built March 1906 for George Crookes of Ackworth in the West Riding of Yorkshire. Note the extra large front tanks fitted to both engines.

McLaren 8nhp compound road engine No 1571, Registration No NC 2305, built July 1919 for James Hill of Manchester. She was acquired by Allen Knight of Huddersfield in the twenties. In 1944 they rebuilt the engine, fitted Pickering governors, a new chimney with a Fowler brass top and new rear wheels which they made from mild steel. After painting and lining she was sold to Herbert Marsh of Blackledge, nr Wigan, in June of that year.

McLaren 10nhp compound road engine No 956, *Nil Desperandum*, Registration No, WR 7390, built in December 1907 for G. & J. Stubley of Batley in the West Riding of Yorkshire. She was bought by Allen Knight & Son (Boilers) Ltd of Huddersfield in 1934. In this picture, taken at their yard in June 1942, Willie Knight, Allen's son, poses with the engine, the year before it was scrapped.

Burrell 7nhp compound road locomotive No 3057, Registration No BE 7217, built December 1908 and sold to W. Smith of North Warnborough, nr Odiham, Hampshire. This photograph taken from a postcard shows her with a load of 9500 bricks. The reverse side of the postcard, addressed to Mr C Burrell & Sons, expresses their satisfaction for the engine sold to them from the show.

Burrell 8nhp compound road engine No 2067, Registration No NR 94, built February 1898 as a showmans engine for John Barker of Norwich and named *City of Norwich*. By 1913 she was owned by Houghton & Cowman of Asfordby, Leicestershire. This photograph was taken at Plumtree, Nottinghamshire, in 1915.

Fowler 7nhp Class R3 compound road locomotive No 15321, Registration No BE 7647, built in January 1919 for the War Department. In this picture, in the ownership of Frank Burgess of Downham Market, she is delivering a new boiler to the Ely Gas Works.

Wallis & Steevens 8nhp single cylinder road locomotive No 2288, Registration No BW 4741, built in 1893 for Kinson Pottery Ltd of Dorset. She was last known to be in the ownership of J.B. Warke & Co of Belfast in 1945.

Wallis & Steevens 10nhp compound road locomotive No 2644 *General Buller*, built 1903 for their Cornish agents, Hosken, Trevithick & Polkinghorn. They delivered it to their customer, G. Carlyn of Truro, who part exchanged it with them in 1911 for a new Wallis & Steevens wagon. This photograph shows the engine on test at the works prior to the canopy being fitted.

Wallis & Steevens 10nhp single cylinder road locomotive No 2336, built March 1895 and sold to W. Cox of Farnham, Surrey. She was later sold to Benfield and Loxley of Oxford. In this photograph taken when new she is complete with three Wallis & Steevens built wagons.

Wallis & Steevens 7nhp single cylinder road locomotive No 2600, *Lawrence*, Registration No HO 5631, built in 1903 and supplied to Neave & Co of Fordingbridge, Hampshire. In 1923 she was sold to W. Everitt of Gussage All Saints, Dorset.

Fowler 8nhp Class B5 'Lion' road locomotive No 8387 *Imperatrix*, Registration No AY 9710, built November 1899 and sold to Mitchells Ltd of Halifax, West Yorkshire. By the year 1916 she had been purchased by Thomas Cowman & Sons of Asfordby, Leicestershire. This picture shows her at Nottingham in that year.

Fowler 6nhp Class A7 compound road locomotive No 12701, Registration No KE 2797, built May 1912 for William Arnold & Sons of Branbridge, Kent. In the 1920s she was purchased by John Botton & Sons of Kent and converted into a showmans engine.

Burrell 6nhp compound road locomotive No 3829, Registration No PB 9687, built March 1920 and sold to T. & W.F. Hooper of Liskeard, Cornwall. By October of the same year she had been bought by the well known boilermakers and heavy haulage contractors, J. Hickey & Sons of Richmond, London.

Ransomes, Sims & Jefferies 6nhp single cylinder crane engine No 31066, Registration No PV 4943, built March 1920 and retained by them for use as their yard engine. She was sold *circa* 1955 to Messrs Harwickes of Ewell, Surrey. Note the power assisted steering operated by utilising the crane drive shaft when disconnected from the crane.

Fowler crane engine No 12749 *Daisy*, Registration No XC 9654, built July 1911 and sold to the London Traction Haulage Co. This photograph was taken at the Royal Show, Ipswich in 1934. She was cut up for scrap at Southampton in 1957.

An official works photograph of Fowler Class B5 compound sprung road locomotive No 9447, built in December 1902 and fitted with front mounted jib crane and side mounted bollard crane. Supplied via Fowlers (Magdeburg) to Austrian Lloyds Navigation.

Fowler Class D2 crane engine No 7940, built June 1900 for Taylor Bros & Co of Leeds. In this view she is lifting a crankshaft casting.

Fowler 7nhp compound Class R1 crane road locomotive No 9385, built in 1903 she was sent to the USA for the World's Fair being held in St Louis. She was returned to the United Kingdom and sold in May 1907 to the Cornish Consolidated Tin Mines.

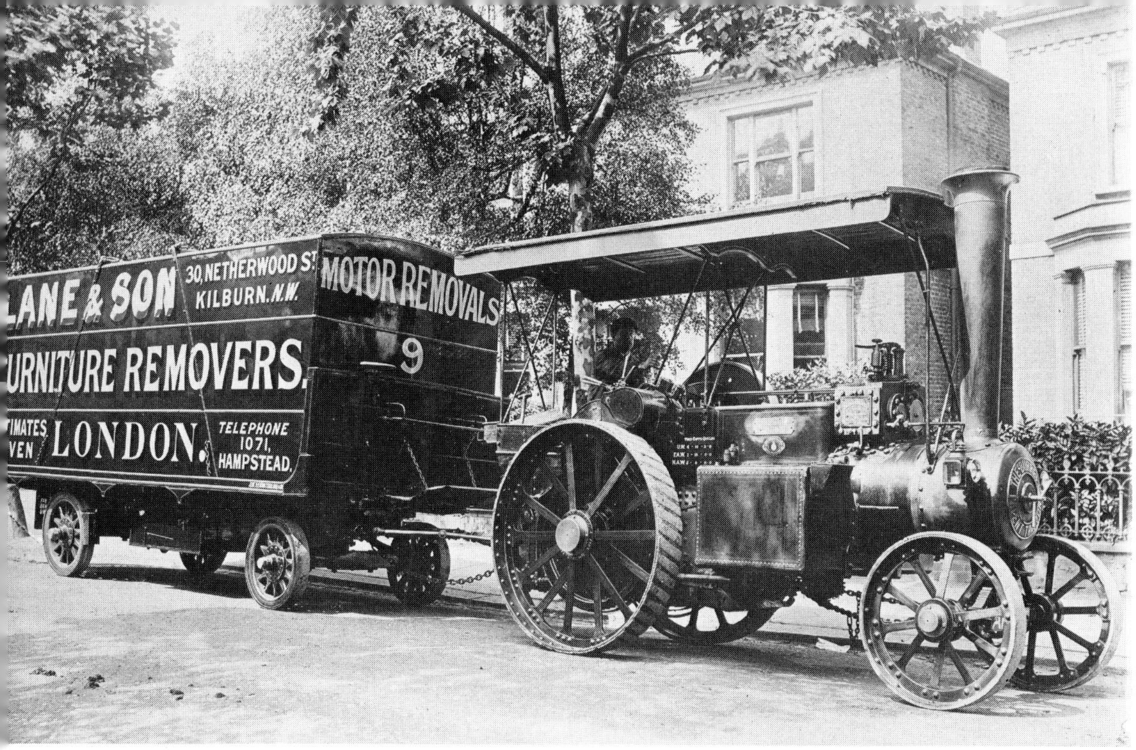

Burrell 5 ton compound tractor No 3064, Registration No AH 026, built December 1908 and sold to Lane & Son of Kilburn, London. In March 1915 she was for sale by auction at Nuneaton, but the new owner was not recorded.

Wallis & Steevens 4¼ ton compound oil bath tractor No 2891, built in 1906 and sold to W.J.W. Pole of Bridgewater, Somerset. They used her for three years before returning her to the works presumably in part exchange for another engine. This photograph shows a typical use for these light tractors with two removal vans. Note the front water tank on top of the smokebox which aided weight distribution.

Marshall 5 ton compound tractor No 59508, Registration No AX 452, built June 1912 and sold to J. & V. Pask of Caerleon, Monmouthshire. In this specially posed photograph she is seen with two trailers loaded with pipes with the proud owners Mr J and Mr V Pask looking on.

A Foden 'D' Type tractor, number unknown, being used on trade plates carting sugar beet. It is more likely that the tractor is being used on a demonstration.

Robey 'Express' tractor No 42922, Registration No FE 8111, built April 1926 and delivered to the East Anglian Roadstone & Transport Co of Norwich. This picture shows her at Ipswich Docks in August 1933.

Foster 'Wellington' tractor No 14066, Registration No FE 1589, built April 1915 and sold to Chas. G. Collis & Co of Kettering. The young man in the photograph, Dick Collis, was eventually to take over the management of the firm. By 1926 she had changed owners for the fifth time and by then had received the new registration No PP 5649.

In 1906 Fowlers built four Class T three cylinder tractors, No 10523 shown above was fitted with Walschaerts valve gear. She was ex-works in July and was sold to F.H. Hawkes of Otley, Yorkshire. Her three sisters Nos 10524, 10525 and 10526 were all fitted with Firth's valve gear, only 10524 remaining in England the other two going for export. They were interesting machines, the engines being enclosed and running in an oilbath which was mounted on top of the Belpaire firebox. The crankshafts were turned from the solid making disc cranks whilst the connecting rods had marine type big ends. No 10524 which was built in December, Registration No U 773 was sold to the Tractor Haulage Co of Bootle, Lancashire. It would seem that she did not come up to their expectations as she was returned to the works within a year. In December 1907 she was sold to Barnby Bendall & Co of Cheltenham in whose ownership she is shown below. In 1908 she broke a valve whilst halfway up the Hogsback Hill with a loaded furniture van.

Wallis & Steevens 4¼ ton compound motor tractor No 2964, Registration No AA 2189, built June 1907, for W.W. Howard, Bros & Co of Fenchurch Street, London. By 1917 she was owned by Travis & Arnold of Sutton Bridge, Lincolnshire and in 1921 received the new Registration No DO 893. She was last licenced in 1938.

Wallis & Steevens 4¼ ton compound oil bath motor tractor No 2853, Registration No AA 2062, built September 1905 and supplied to the stores department of the General Post Office at their Mount Pleasant depot in London. Note the royal cypher on the side of the boiler and the side lamp mounted on the gear casing.

Foden timber tractor No 13494, Registration No OU 5864, built June 1930 and supplied new to T. Mossop & Co Ltd. This is a typical view of a tractor at work, note the earthing chain hanging beneath the engine. No 13494 survived until 1945 when she was sent to the breaker's yard.

Foden tractor No 13802, Registration No VN 2912, built August 1931 for the North Riding County Council, with whom she spent the whole of her working life. She, too, carries an earthing chain hanging from the water pump suction pipe.

Nearside and offside official works photographs of Fowler Class T1 5 ton tractor No 11023, Registration No U 827. Built in April 1908 and sold to Wintle & Sons of Ross-on-Wye, Herefordshire. Note the smooth rear wheel surfaces.

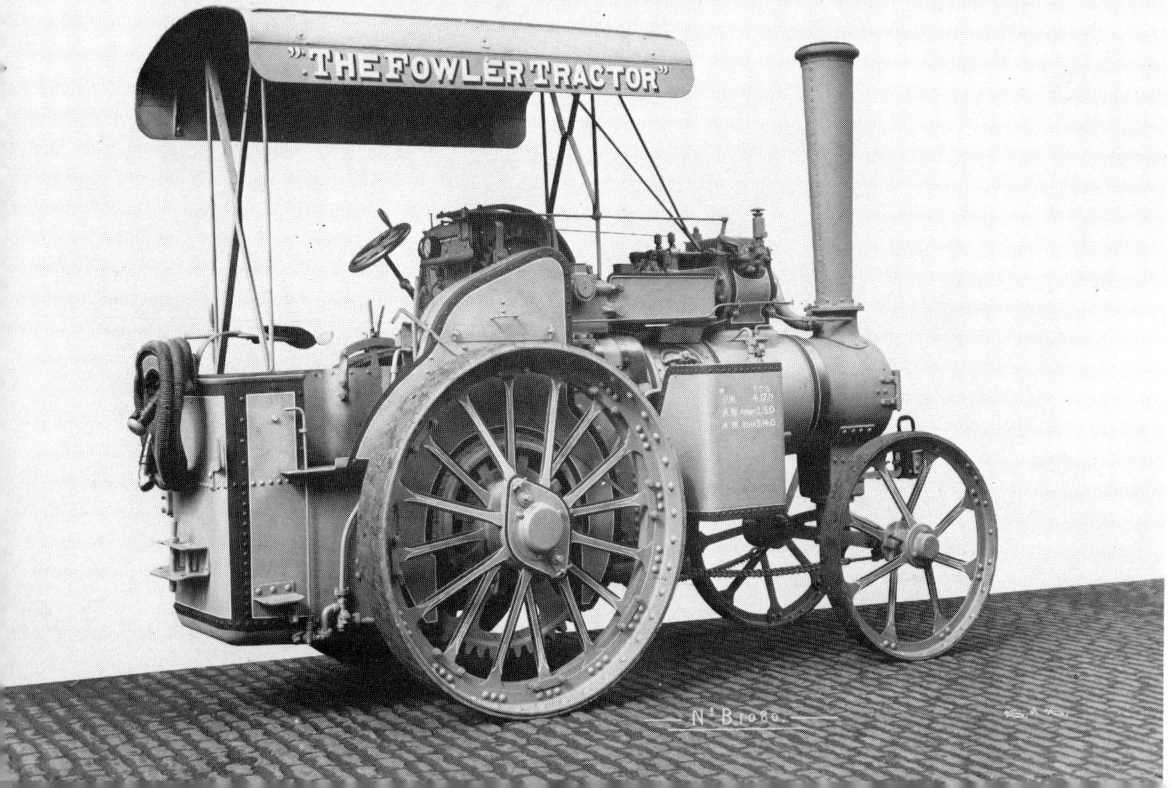

Wallis & Steevens 3 ton single cylinder motor tractor No 2620, supplied new in 1902 to Reading Workmans Coal Union. It was reported as being for sale some years later with Reading dealer, Henry Lewis Senior.

Wallis & Steevens 2hp single cylinder motor tractor No 2451, supplied new in 1898 to Rebora Bros, of Brique, Switzerland. This engine was fitted with a boiler feed pump driven from an eccentric mounted behind the flywheel on the crankshaft. The pump is visible behind the bottom left quarter of the rear wheel. Parts to convert her to a steam roller were sent to Switzerland in 1909.

Fowler 3nhp Class T3 compound tractor No 14412, Registration No U 4662, built June 1918 for J.W. Harris & Son of Hook Norton, Oxfordshire. By 1935 she had been converted to a showmans tractor and was owned by A. Greenway of Braintree, Essex. This photograph shows her taking water on the outskirts of Ipswich in August 1936.

Burrell 6nhp compound road locomotive No 3847, Registration No EB 3035. Built July 1920 and sold to R. Drake & Co of Sutton Ely. Circa 1933 she was bought by J. Barker & Sons of Ipswich by which time she had been converted to a showmans engine, named *Princess Marina*, and re-registered receiving the new number CL 4483. This picture shows her at the Foxhall Road Fairground, Ipswich in 1933.

Wallis & Steevens 7nhp compound showmans engine No 7125 *King of the Road*, Registration No KE 3048, built September 1909 for Mrs J. Pettigrove of Orpington, Kent. She finished her working life with showman T. Drakeley of Birmingham and was cut up by Birds of Stratford-upon-Avon in 1952. Note the early Dickinson dynamo.

Wallis & Steevens 6nhp compound showmans engine No 7052 *Morning Star*, Registration No R 6043, built July 1908 for W. Cole of Yate, Gloucestershire. She passed into the ownership of H. Freeman of Merthyr Tydfil, Wales who renamed her *Pride of Merthyr*, she finished her working life with Mrs Oadley of Alfreton, Derbyshire and was last licenced in 1947.

The Fowler B6

Fowler B6 'Super Lion' showmans engine No 19782 *Lion*, Registration No UB 9763, built March 1932 for Anderton & Rowland of Bristol. Note the non-standard chimney top, twisted brass on steering and brake spindles, water lifter on off-side front tank wheels finished in maroon, brass stars and rings on the motion covers. Brass moulded boiler bands, works plate fitted to near-side of boiler cleading. Brass stars on front tanks, fitted with oil lamps only.

In the early twenties Harold Livesey, Fowler's works manager left them due to a disagreement with Mr Charles Fowler and obtained the position of general manager with Charles Burrell & Sons Ltd.

By now Burrells were members of A.G.E. (Agricultural and General Engineers) and whilst a friendly attachment grew up between him and Sydney Harrison, Burrells sales manager, Harold Livesey grew less and less appreciative of A.G.E. methods and after only a few months he left Burrells and went back to John Fowlers.

Sidney Harrison could see the way things were progressing with the A.G.E. concern and when Harold Livesey made overtures for him to join the Leeds firm he did not hesitate and so early in June 1928 he severed his connections with the firm he had joined in September 1900 as an apprentice and went over to his competitors, John Fowler & Co (Leeds) Ltd.

His knowledge of the Burrell product and more importantly his intimate friendship with the showland users of Burrell engines proved a great asset. With the ready collaboration of the late Alf Pepper of Fowlers with whom, although a competitor, he had over a number of years become increasingly friendly enabled the four Super Lions to be built with many modifications from the Fowler traditions, not least being the fitting of left hand steering gear to meet the demands of his old Burrell customers.

Fowler B6 'Super Lion' showmans engine No 19783 *King Carnival II*, Registration No EF 4883, built April 1932 for Frank McConville of West Hartlepool, Cleveland. Note no twisted brass on steering or brake spindles, water lifter on off-side front tank, wheels finished in yellow, no brass stars or rings on motion covers, flat brass boiler bands, works plate fitted to near-side of boiler cleading. No brass stars on front tanks, fitted with oil lamps only.

Super Lions

Fowler B6 'Super Lion' showmans engine No 19989 *Onward*, Registration No XG 2010, built April 1933 for Samuel Ingham of Hyde, Cheshire. Note: No twisted brass on steering or brake spindles, water lifter on off-side front tank, wheels finished in yellow, no stars or rings on motion covers, brass moulded boiler bands, works plate fitted to near-side of boiler cleading, no brass stars on front tanks, fitted with oil lamps only.

The four illustrations show the detail differences between the engines and the following information from Sidney Harrison's sales notebook in the author's collection sets out the prices and options available to the purchaser of a Super Lion showmans engine in those days.

Twisted brass pillars and knobs for awning with cross stays and diagonals £25.00
Twisted brass for steerage and brake spindles £4.00
Brass caps for front and rear wheels £9.00
ditto third motion shaft £1.00
ditto flywheel £1.00
ditto steerage and brake handwheels £10.00
Cylinder covers, stars and lagging £5.00
Brass mouldings for boiler barrel and manhole £8.00
Brass stars on sides of front tanks £3.00
Brass stars and rings on motion covers £5.00
Brass ring on flywheel £3.00
Brass dome for steerage worm and wheel £3.00
Brass guard over pump £1.00
Extra set of water gauge fittings £4.00
Electric lighting, including generator, switchbox, two head lamps, tail lamp and inspection lamp £35.00

Specification

B6, 10hp Super Lion compound loco with three speeds, oil bath spring gear, special front spring, twin endless solid tyres to hind wheels, singles to fronts, gear driven pump, injector, Pickering governors, rim brakes, large front tank, winding drum with 75 yards rope, liner in smokebox, splashers over cranks, large size big end lubricators, dynamo bracket and platform, wide, long awning with side and end curtains, extension chimney, flywheel brake, Rochester 3 pint lubricator, polished copper pipes, special painting and lining

Price £1,470.00
Special car lifting crane with pole etc £48.00

Fowler B6 'Super Lion' showmans engine No 20223 *Supreme*, Registration No EU 5313, built March 1934 for Mrs A Deakin & Sons of Brynmawr, Brecon. Note: Twisted brass, chromium plated on steering and brake spindles, water lifter on near-side front tank, wheels finished in yellow, brass stars and rings (chromium plated on motion covers), brass, chromium plated, moulded boiler bands, works plate fitted to off-side of boiler cleading, no brass stars on front tanks, fitted with both electric and oil lighting. The chain drive to the generator can be seen just to the left of the motion cover plate.

Burrell 10nhp single crank compound showmans engine No 1845 *The Dutchman*, built August 1895 for William Symonds of Gloucester who used her until sold out of showland in 1916.

Burrell 8nhp compound showmans engine No 2650, *Independent*, Registration No DH 2479, built February 1904 for Ralph & Pedley of Northampton. In 1907 she was sold to Patrick Collins of Bloxwich who re-named her *Mark Twain*.

Burrell 8nhp compound showmans engine No 2877 *His Majesty*, Registration No HT 3163, built February 1907 for Charles Heal & Sons of Glastonbury. She worked the whole of her commercial life with this well-known firm until being sold for preservation in 1959. This photograph was taken at Taunton Fair in 1938.

Burrell 8nhp compound showmans engine No 3949 *Princess Mary*, Registration No NO 8287, built February 1923 and sold to W. Nichols of Forest Gate, Essex. She was exhibited on Burrells stand at the Smithfield Show in 1922. This photograph was taken at Chingford Plain Fair on Easter Sunday 1957 whilst owned by Charles Presland of Tilbury, Essex. She was not being used for generating electricity acting as a reserve but used for pulling his loads.

Burrell 7nhp compound showmans engine No 3072, *Shakespeare*, Registration No J 6838, built February 1909 for Wadbrook & Scard of Fulham, London. By 1920 she was with John Hoadley of Wallsend-on-Tyne and renamed *Daisy*.

Burrell 8nhp compound showmans engine No 3833, *Queen Mary*, Registration No BR 1498, built May 1920 for Alf Payne of York. She was sold in 1923 to Anderton & Rowland of Bristol with whom she spent the next twenty years, being sold in 1943 to her last showland owner Mrs Symonds of Gloucester. This photograph was taken at Bridgewater Fair in October 1942.

Foden Showmans Engines

Foden 6nhp compound showmans engine No 1142, *Sally*, built October 1906 for Hackney Bros of Preston, Lancashire. Sometime later she was sold to Carrick Wilmot of Glasgow and although she changed owners a number of times she remained with Scottish showmen for the rest of her working life.

Foden 6nhp compound showmans engine No 1540, *Prince Llewellyn*, Registration No FE 4204, built March 1908 and sold to Mrs Simons & Son of Caernarvon and Leicester. *Circa* 1916 she passed into the ownership of Hill Bros of Bedminster, Bristol. At a later date not recorded she was bought by Charles Ling of Doncaster and re-named *Duchess of York.*

Foden 6nhp compound showmans engine No 2106 *Dreadnought*, Registration No, BN 4916, built May 1910 for Simons & Greatorex of Nantwich, Cheshire. She changed owners a number of times during her working life finally being scrapped in Scotland in 1939. Note the water lifter and large front water tank fitted to the left side of the engine. Detail differences to the tenders and brake winding shafts are worthy of note.

Foster 65bhp showmans engine No 14405 *William Henry*, Registration No WA 5519, built October 1921 for J.E. Whiting of Owlerton, Sheffield. She was sold to Pat Collins of Bloxwich in March 1927. The works number was changed to 14446 and the registration number became DH 4593 and she was re-named *The Leader*. This picture was taken at Leicester Fair in 1956.

Foster 65bhp showmans engine No 13052, *Clara*, Registration No DH 2477, built April 1913 and sold to Pat Collins of Bloxwich. It is reputed that this was the last showmans engine to travel in Lancashire. This photograph was taken at Denton Fair in 1941.

Burrell 8hp compound showmans engine No 2351 *Ephraim*, Registration No AL 9309, built February 1901 and supplied to F. & J. Cox of Codnor, Derbyshire. In this view taken at Long Eaton, Nottinghamshire in 1907 Fred Cox stands by the rear wheel. Note the small belly tank and the screw jack under the rear wheel to stop excessive rocking too and fro whilst generating.

Fowler 8hp Class B6 compound showmans engine No 11987 *Violet Victoria*, supplied new to J. Murphy of Newcastle on the 30th March 1910. Driver Jack Ellis and steersman Jack Wilson are happy to pose for the camera. A second dynamo (exciter) has been mounted on the belly tank.

Fowler 8nhp Class B6 compound showmans engine No 14119, *The Great Bear*, Registration No DP 6655, built in January 1915 she was delivered to the War Department. *Circa* 1925 she was purchased by the well known engine dealers Charles Openshaw of Reading, who converted her into a showmans engine and sold her to Joseph Ling & Sons of Doncaster for travelling his set of steam yachts.

Burrell 8nhp compound showmans engine No 3547, *Tucker*, Registration No FT 643, built February 1914 and supplied new to the executors of William Murphy of Newcastle-upon-Tyne when it carried the name *Amy*. This picture shows her having suffered the indignity of a broken back axle in June 1933. By this time she had been fitted with a crane tower.

These two illustrations are of Fowler 7nhp compound road locomotive Class R3 No 15657 *Kitchener*, Registration No FX 6661. The top view shows her in the ownership of F.J. Barnes Ltd of Portland, Dorset, to whom she was supplied new in September 1920, and used for bringing the stone from the quarry down to Portland Harbour returning with the empty wagons. In 1932 *Kitchener* was sold and returned to Fowler's works at Leeds where she was converted into a showmans engine. She was acquired by showlady Mrs H. Oadley of Alfreton, in Derbyshire. The illustration below shows her in June 1952 just after she had been sold out of showland for preservation.

urrell 8nhp compound howmans engine No 2723 *oris,* Registration No HT 468, built March 1905 and old to James Leo of Preston, ancashire. In 1908 she was old to Marshall Hill of ristol and renamed *Bristol ity.* She survived until 1950 hen sold for scrap.

urrell 8nhp compound howmans engine No 4038 *nglands Glory,* Registration o PR 6162, built January 926 and sold to Bath & ortland Stone Firms Ltd. In 932 she was sold to Charles leal & Sons of Glastonbury, omerset who converted her ito a showmans engine. In iis photograph she is seen t Taunton Fair in 1937.

owler 7nhp compound road ocomotive Class R3 No 3468 *My Lady of Kent,* egistration No KE 3384, uilt March 1914 for Kent laulage Co Ltd of Hoo treet, Werburgh. She had iany different owners and omes ranging from righton, Leicester and ucknell until being urchased by G. Rogers & ons of Chipping Sodbury in loucestershire in 1932 who onverted her into a howmans engine. She was old again in 1936 to Sam mart of Bedminster, Bristol ho re-named her *Queen lary.*

Burrell 8nhp compound showmans engine No 3443 *Lord Nelson*, Registration No CO 3822, built February 1913 for Anderton and Rowland of Bristol. Sold in 1943 to Hardiman and Strong (trading as John Cole) of Bristol. In this photograph, taken in August 1935, she is seen leaving Paignton Fairground.

Burrell 5nhp compound showmans engine No 3669 *Nero*, Registration No G 6470, built July 1915 for E.H Bostock of Glasgow. Two engines were used by this firm for travelling their circus *Nero* and her companion *Rajah*, so named after the two lions in the show. The back of *Rajah* is just visible in this photograph taken at Calne, Wiltshire in April 1931.

Burrell 8nhp compound showmans engine no 2898 *Victoria*, Registration No SG 7107, built April 1907 for W. Taylor of Ilkeston, Derbyshire. Sold in 1915 to John Cole of Bristol and re-named *King Cole*, *circa* 1919 she was bought by John Evans of Edinburgh.

Burrell 8nhp compound showmans engine No 2072 *The Masterpiece*, Registration No AD 8786, built March 1898 and supplied to John Cole of Staple Hill, Bristol.

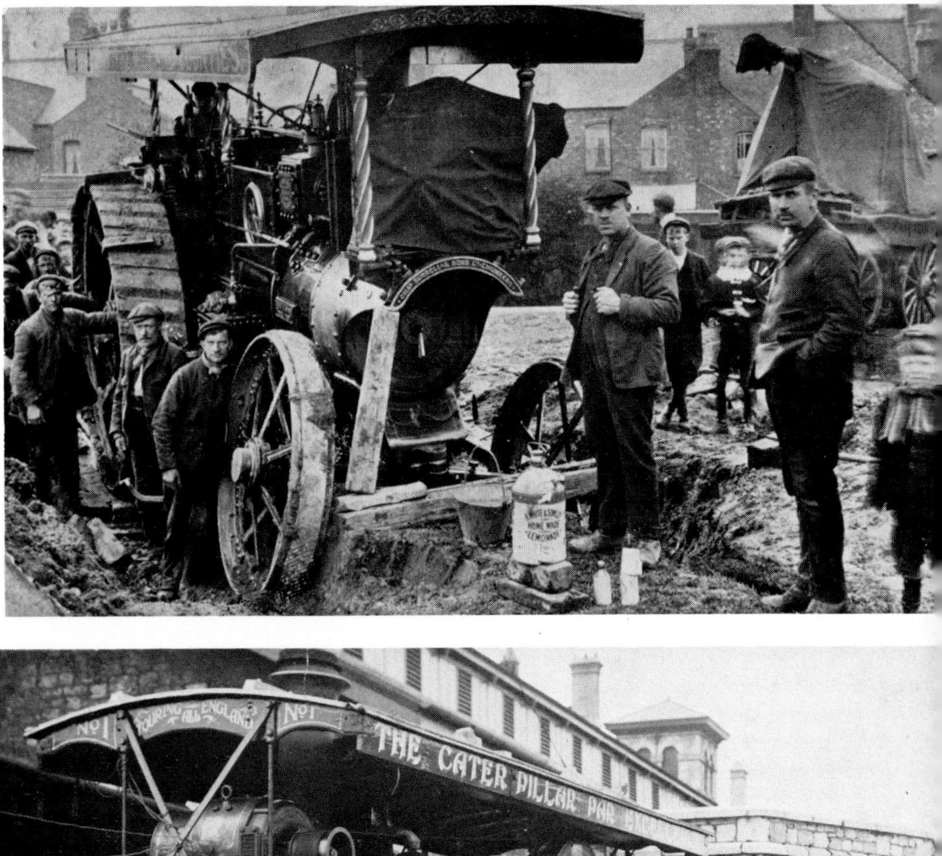

Burrell 8nhp two speed compound showmans engine No 1999 *Victoria*, Registration No AN 2364, built May 1897. This view taken at Nuneaton, Warwickshire, in 1914 shows the type of problems the showman had to contend with. Wet weather would turn the fairground into a quagmire with the result that as soon as the engines tried to manoeuvre they would very often sink in up to the ashpan. Note the large jar of A. White & Sons Ltd, home made lemonade.

urrell 7nhp compound howmans engine No 089 *His Majesty*, egistration No CK 3347, uilt March 1909 for ohn Green of Preston ancashire. This hotograph taken at ewton Abbot in Devon hows the engine when ouring all England with heir caterpillar ride. heir well known driver, he late Tommy Glover, seen standing fourth rom the right.

Fowler 14nhp single cylinder ploughing engines Nos 3160 and 3161, Registration Nos EW 2176 and EW 2177, built in June 1877 and supplied to Dean & Adamson of Cottenham, Cambridgeshire. They received new boilers in 1912 and finished their days with How Bros of Leighton, Huntingdonshire.

A Fowler single cylinder horizontal shaft ploughing engine deposited in the River Ivel as a result of the bridge collapsing at Broom, near Biggleswade, in Bedfordshire on February 11th 1873. The rather aloof gentleman on the left of the group could well be the owner of the engine reflecting on the sudden fame brought about by the accident.

A delightful pair of photographs showing a set of ploughing tackle on the road just after the turn of the century. It is thought that the engines are numbers 2456 *(above)* and 2457 *(below)*. They are 14nhp single cylinder engines with tank steering gear built in January 1875. Neither engine has a lagged boiler. They were new to J.H. Hawkins, of Ellenthorpe, Yorkshire.

Burrell 16nhp single crank compound ploughing engines No 2889, Registration No CE 8372 *(above)* and No 2890, Registration No CE 8371 *(below)*.

Burrell 20nhp 'Universal' ploughing engine undergoing a steam test at the Burrell works at Thetford, Norfolk prior to completion. The boiler lagging and front tool box have still to be fitted before entry into the paint shop.

Burrell 'Universal' Ploughing Engines

(left and bottom right)
Burrell 16nhp single crank compound 'Universal' ploughing engines Nos 2889 right hand engine and No 2890 left hand engine. With this system a large vertical winding drum is affixed to one side of the boiler and driven from a pinion on the crankshaft. Beneath the tender at the rear of the engine is a large diameter pulley round which the rope is led off to the implement. One of the advantages claimed for this system by the makers was that the need for coiling gear was eliminated, so reducing both friction and maintenance. These two engines were built in April 1907 and supplied new to George Flack of Orwell, near Royston, Hertfordshire.

Fowler 8nhp Class T1 single cylinder double drum ploughing engine No 8204, built February 1899 and sold to Captain E.W. Baird of Exning, Suffolk. These photographs were taken at Acton, in Suffolk in 1956 whilst in the ownership of W.F. Bear shortly before being cut up for scrap. Note the double drum ploughing gear and the extended pivot point for the front axle.

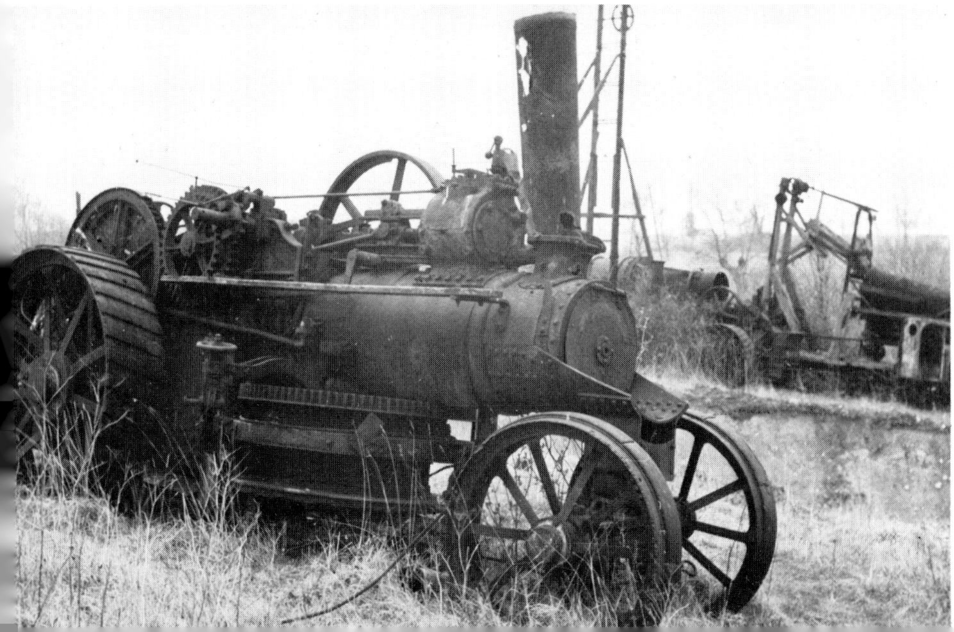

Fowler single cylinder 14nhp ploughing engine built *circa* 1875, Registration No NR 1212. The maker's number of this engine will probably never be known as many different numbers have been found stamped on different parts indicating that she has been made up from a number of engines at the time she was reboilered by Allens of Oxford. This photograph was taken in 1959 during a cultivating demonstration whilst this engine was still being used commercially by Beeby Bros of Rempstone, Nottinghamshire.

Fowler 16nhp Class BB compound ploughing engine No 14384, Registration No NM 1283, built August 1917. In this late fifties' photograph she is seen cultivating when owned by John Patten of Little Hadham, Herts.

Two early single cylinder Fowler ploughing engines complete with harrow and water cart pose for the photographer whilst working at Belstead Hall, near Ipswich *circa* 1901.

Burrell 8nhp single cylinder ploughing engine No 776, built June 1879, the sister engine 777 can be seen in the background. These engines were new to R.G. Wilberforce of Woolavington, West Sussex. This picture was taken when they were in the ownership of E. & W. Morley of Brize Norton.

Fowler 12nhp Class B4 ploughing engine No 12407 *Napoleon*, Registration No NK 935. Built August 1912 and fitted with double speed ploughing gear. This engine paired with No 12406 *Wellington*, were supplied new to A. T. Oliver & Sons of Wandon End, Luton, Bedfordshire and was their No 2 set.

Fowler 16nhp Class BB1 ploughing engine No 15190, Registration No NK 931, built July 1918 and sold to A. T. Oliver & Sons of Wandon End, Luton. Driver A. Wilmot and steersman J. Eatwell pause in their duties and pose for the photographer *circa* 1920.
In the rear can be seen the sister engine No 15191, Registration No NK 932 with the cultivator and plough in tow.

The Howard 'Farmers Engine'

The original Howard 'Farmers Engine' was introduced at the Taunton Agricultural Show in 1875. At the Carlisle Show in 1880 they presented their modified engine which incorporated a number of improvements. The example shown opposite and below, now in the Henry Ford Museum at Michigan, USA, was worked by Baldwin Bros of Wadhurst, Sussex between 1916 and 1922. It then stood out of use until purchased by the museum and sent to the USA in 1929. The design has many features in its favour, such as the use of simple spur gearing for driving both the road wheels and the ploughing windlass. The winding drums were attached to their own sub-frame thus relieving the boiler from stress. The engine being located inside the tender alongside the driver facilitated the job of oiling and inspection. For heavy boiler or firebox repairs the tender could be unbolted from the boiler enabling the latter to be sent away for attention, this eliminated having to remove the drum and gearing, flywheel and motion as would be necessary on the more orthodox design. Whilst designed with ploughing as its prime function it was possible at the end of the ploughing season to remove the windlass and so reduce the overall weight to that of a normal traction engine enabling it to undertake other duties around the farm. Alas, in spite of these advantages, relatively few engines were built and they were never able to compete with the by now accepted Fowler design.

A rare photograph of a Howard 8nhp 'Farmers Engine' taken in China towards the end of the last century.

Howard 8nhp single cylinder double drum 'Farmers Engine' of 1877, Registration No CE 8721. This engine was supplied new to a Mr Stevenson of Burwell, Cambridgeshire, and was worked until 1928. She was then bought back by Howards of Bedford to prevent it going to the Henry Ford Museum in Dearborn, Michigan, USA. She was driven back to Bedford under its own steam only to be left standing in their yard. When the firm was taken over the new owners had no interest in the old relic and she was cut up *circa* 1930. Luckily the Ford Museum located another engine down in Sussex which they purchased. This photograph was taken at Burwell in 1927.

Oxford Steam Ploughing Company rebuilt engine No 57, new in 1910 to J.P. Grundy of Barton Seagrave, Northamptonshire. In 1920 she was rebuilt again with piston valve cylinder and given a new number 75, Registration No BD 5585. This photograph was taken in 1955 when she belonged to Smith of Wymington, Bedfordshire. The scrap man had supplied her to replace Fowler ploughing engine No 14709 which they had cut up in error.

Fowler 14nhp single cylinder ploughing engine No 2144, built September 1873 for Mr W.C. Dixon of Camberwell, London. This picture was taken in the 1920s when owned by Mr Fretingham of Radcliffe-on-Trent, Nottinghamshire.

Unfortunately no details are available of this interesting picture of an early Aveling & Porter single cylinder ploughing engine. A point of interest is the horizontal cross shaft steering gear.

On this and the opposite page are six pictures of a very interesting old ploughing engine standing at Gamlingay in Cambridgeshire in 1957 where it was used for sterilising soil. Within a few weeks of taking these photographs it was cut up for scrap.
Built in August 1876, Fowler No 3049 was a single cylinder 14nhp ploughing engine, Registration No CE 7698, which, together with her sister engine No 3048, was delivered to H. & C. Roberts of Haynes in Bedfordshire. Later in their lives they passed into the ownership of well known ploughing contractors Messrs Pamplin Bros of Cherry Hinton, Cambridgeshire. Whilst in their ownership they were converted to compounds by fitting Burrell single crank compound cylinders and motion.
Circa 1941 they were purchased by another contractor, S.A. Flack of Orwell, also in Cambridgeshire. By this time they must have been nearing the end of their useful working lives as ploughing engines and sometime probably in the fifties 3049 was sold to a customer at Gamlinghay for sterilising duties whilst the fate of her sister is unknown.

(Top) Gear-side view showing the very neat manner in which the conversion had been carried out. The winding drum no longer required for sterilising duties has been removed.

(Centre) Close up of the Burrell cylinder block and motion. Note the second speed gear in its place on the footboard.

(Bottom) The gearing and massive crankshaft and big end.

The rear view with the name of Pamplin Bros just discernable on the rear of the tender, access to which was by the the three steps shown as it did not have a cut-out in the side.

Another view of the Burrell motion and cylinder block.

The regulator linkage and the control rod for admitting high pressure steam into the low pressure cylinder for starting. The lever for engaging the ploughing gear is also shown.

Aveling & Porter 14nhp ploughing engines Nos 8890 and 8891 *Field Marshall Haig* and *General Byng*, Registration Nos DO 1943 and DO 1944. These engines were supplied new in 1917 to F.H. Cooke of Spalding, Lincs. This pair of engines complete with implements, living van and water cart were advertised for sale in the *Farmer and Stockbreeder* during June 1958, luckily they were purchased for preservation by George Cushing of Thursford in Norfolk.

Top right
Aveling & Porter 30nhp compound ploughing engine Class ZRSD No 7380, built June 1911 and sold with sister engine No 7379 to a customer in Turkey. She is fitted with governors and two speed ploughing gear.

Bottom right
Aveling & Porter compound ploughing engine Class ZTD No 8912 *John Bull*, Registration No NO 3606, built July 1918 for Kirby & Co of Southminster, Essex fitted with governors and two-speed ploughing gear.

Middle left
This view from the footplate of No 8890 shows the two wheels used to operate the gear changing mechanism.

Left
Apart from the rampant horse and Invicta badges on the smoke box door, the curved spokes in the steering wheel and the large casing over the gearing are sure aids to recognition.

JOHN BULL

The unique two-part vertical fire tube boiler fitted with 108 1½ inch diameter tubes. Superheated steam was supplied at a working pressure of 225lbs per square inch. (15.82 KgF/CM^{3})

View through the driver's doorway showing the handbrake operating mechanism, the regulator handle and the traction engine type steering wheel.

Fowler gully emptier No 16576, Registration No KU 8905, built June 1926 and supplied new to the Bradford Corporation cleansing department, their fleet No 6. Many of these wagons had very short lives, quite a few being returned to the works after only two years to be broken up for scrap.

Foden Class E 6 wheel three-way tipper No 13344, Registration No DV 1147, built June 1929 and supplied to Stoneycombe Lime and Stone Co Ltd of Newton Abbot, Devon. In this posed view she is on Foden's trade plates 153M.

Foden 6 ton tipper No 12886, Registration No TU 7761, new in March 1928 to Bethell & Sons of Sale, Cheshire in who's ownership she remained until 1941. In this attractive photograph she is seen having just returned from recovering their Aveling & Porter tandem roller which has a nasty crack through the headstock which has been wired up.

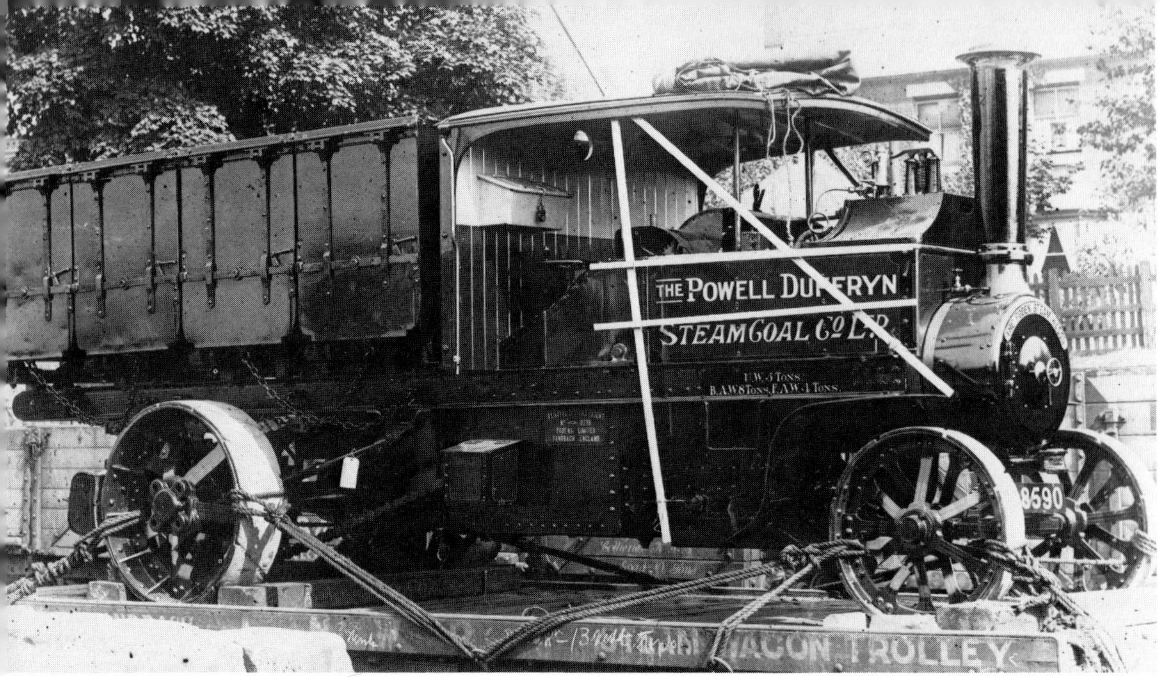

Foden 4 ton wagon No 6238, Registration No M 8590, built August 1916 and supplied to the Powell Duffryn Steam Coal Co Ltd, New Tredegar, South Wales. This photograph shows her being loaded onto a London & North Western 'Steam Wagon Trolley' for despatch to New Tredegar. In 1929 she was fitted with the engine from No 8276. She was scrapped in 1936.

Foden Speed-Six steam wagon No 13656, Registration No JA 1020, supplied new in May 1930 to R. Morten & Son Ltd of Stockport, Lancashire. This series of wagons suffered problems with their boilers so much so that 13656 had replacements in February 1931 and again in September 1934. One wonders when looking at the chimney just in front of the load of cotton waste what reaction would be forthcoming from the insurance companies today.

Foden 6 ton wagon No 13044 *Eveling*, Registration No MP 5938, built July 1928 for E. & J. Fountain of Uxbridge, Middlesex. This photograph shows her in the ownership of Northern Taroads of Kendal and was taken near Appleby, Westmorland.

Foden 5 ton wagon No 10000, Registration No MA 3651, built June 1920 and supplied to the Great Northern Railway, their fleet No 4007.

Foden 5 ton wagon No 785, Registration No CD 267, built August 1904 and supplied new to C.R. Smith & Sons Ltd. Fitted with wood block brakes on the rear wheels and ¾ length canopy.

Foden 5 ton wagon No 745 *Pride of the Midlands*, Registration No BD 112, built April 1904 and supplied new to Walker Soames. Steersman was provided with a seat. Fitted with ½ length canopy.

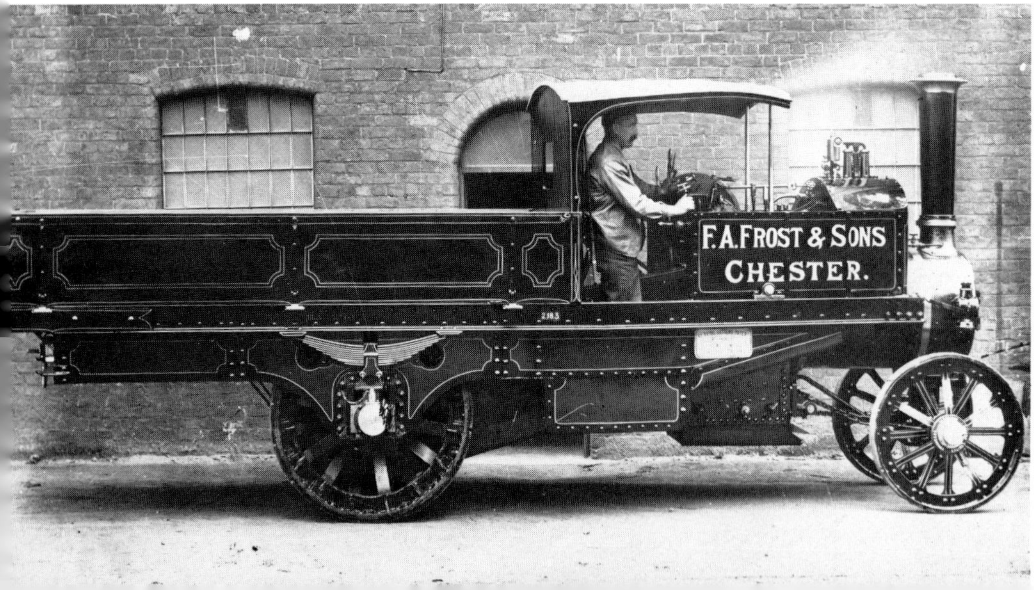

Foden 5 ton wagon No 801, Registration No M 604, built August 1904 and supplied new to F.A. Frost & Sons. Makers could see no reason why the driver should not stand as they did on traction engines.

Foden 5 ton wagon No 8744, Registration No MA 344, built April 1919 and supplied new to W. Astley of Nelson, Lancs. This wagon is fitted with body shield on the driver' side as well as the normal one for the steersman. By October 1927 it had been scrapped.

Foden 3 ton wagon No 8800, Registration No MA 353, built May 1919 and supplied new to Isleworth Brewery, Middlesex. Their fleet No 4, it was scrapped in 1936.

Foden 3 ton wagon No 8850, Registration No MA 738, built June 1919 for the Hexham Rural District Council, Northumberland. By 1933 its working days were over and it was lying derelict.

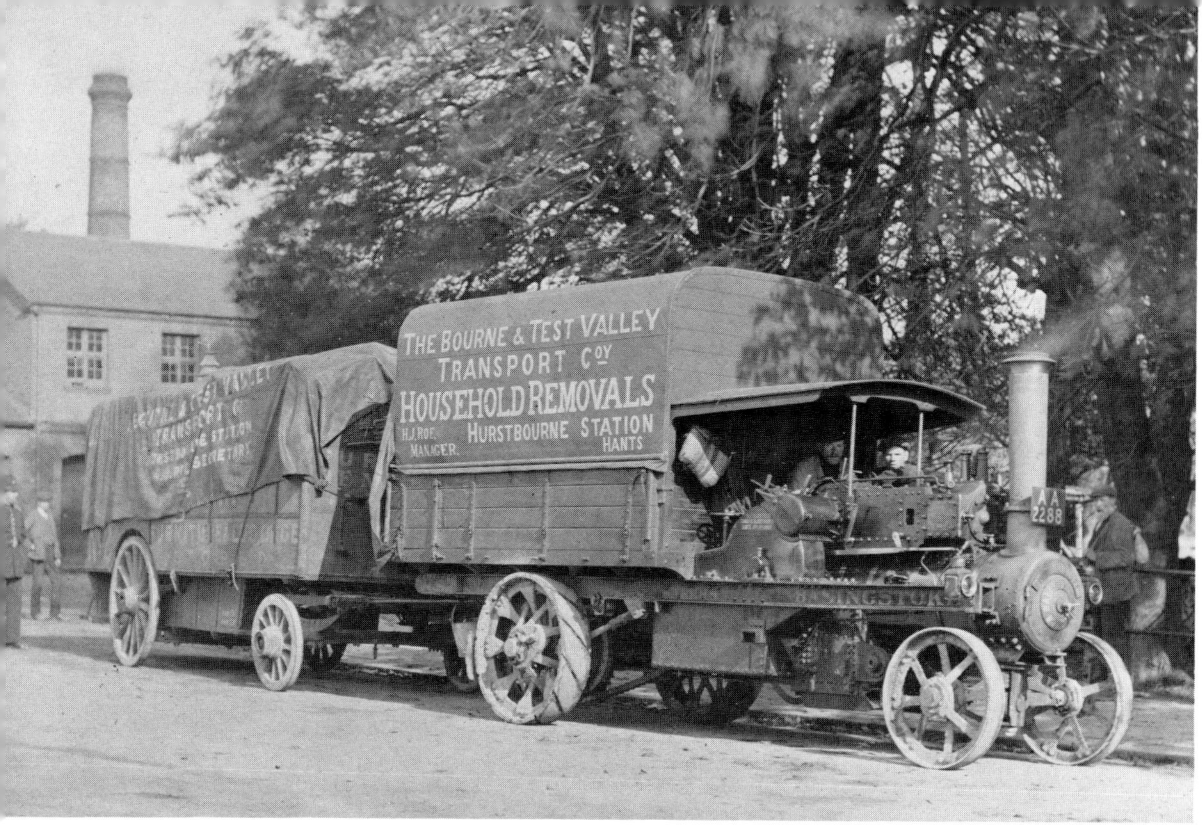

Wallis & Steevens 5 ton oil bath wagon No 7067 *Southern Queen*, Registration No AA 2288, built April 1909 and sold to the Bourne & Test Valley Transport Company of Whitchurch, Hampshire. She finished her working days in George Taylor's scrapyard at Redbourn in Hertfordshire.

Wallis & Steevens 5 ton oil bath high sided tipping wagon No 7337, Registration No AA 5056, built October 1912 and sold to Alfred Schofield of Sheffield. By 1920 they were advertising her for sale.

Wallis & Steevens 3 ton 'Light Type' 3 speed compound wagon on steel wheels No 7316, Registration No AA 5010, built July 1912 and sold to Crouchers Ltd, of Newport, Isle of Wight. In December 1913 she was returned to the works who sold her eventually to Associated Coal Consumers Ltd, London.

Wallis & Steevens 5 ton 'Heavy Type' oil bath compound wagon No 2940, Registration No AA 2197, built July 1907 for Thomas & Evans, *Western Hills Lemonade* of Porth, Glamorgan, their fleet No 4.

Garrett 6 ton superheated wagon No 34932 fitted with a three way tipping body. Registration No SX 2395, built August 1926 and delivered to William Aitken of Stockbridge, Hampshire. In September of the following year she was sold to the Devon County Council (Northern Division) where she spent the rest of her working life. This wagon was one of the last batch built by Garretts and featured Ackerman steering and twin semi-elliptic front springs, details of which show up well in this illustration.

Garrett 5 ton superheated wagon No 31524, Registration No BJ 1794, built August 1913 for the Great Northern Railway Company, their fleet No 3050 and based in the Manchester District. These early wagons were fitted with a centrally pivoted front axle mounted on a transverse spring with chain steering and wooden artillery wheels with steel tyres fitted.

Garrett 8 ton wagon No 34751, Registration No PE 4772, built July 1925 and sold complete with matching trailer to the Fullers Earth Union Ltd, of Redhill, Surrey, with whom she spent the whole of her working life.

Garrett 5 ton superheated wagon No 30376, Registration No BJ 1332, built May 1912 and supplied to the Express Motor Transport Co of Pershore, Worcestershire. According to the records she was never owned by the brewery and as the last part of the town 'Pershore' can just be seen on the side board of the body it must be assumed that she was on long term hire to Showells Brewery Co Ltd.

Burrell 5 ton compound wagon No 3654, Registration No AH 0242, built March 1915 and delivered to Robertson Bros of Woking, Surrey. By May of the same year they had sold it to W.E. Harding of Shrewsbury who were to use it for nine years before selling it to W.E. Chivers & Sons Ltd of Devizes, Wiltshire who retained it for the rest of its working life. She was last licenced in 1924.

Burrell 5 ton compound wagon No 3362, Registration No AH 080, built February 1912, and delivered to A. Adams & Son, of St Albans, Hertfordshire. They sold it to Hill & Partners although the date of this transaction is not recorded, but by December 1921 it was in the hands of J. Wood of Ellesmere, Salop.

Burrell 5 ton compound wagon No 3592, Registration No AH 0106, built November 1912 and sold to M. Williams, Higher Bebington, Cheshire.

Foden 5 ton compound wagon No 971, Registration No M 926, built September 1905 and sold to J. & R. Hutchinson of Nottingham. By 1921 she was owned by Robert Theodore (seen in photograph) of Leicester, who was both a showman and haulage contractor. By removing the caravan body from the wagon he was then ready to operate his haulage business. She had two more owners before retirement. She was last licenced in 1928.

Burrell 5 ton compound wagon No 3373, Registration No AH 078, built April 1912 and delivered to W. Marriage of Warminster, Wiltshire. This postcard photograph addressed to Messrs Chas. Burrell, Thetford, Norfolk, has no other communication upon it, but the postmark, April 29th, would suggest this was one of its first outings when it dropped through the weighbridge. The dress and tough footwear of the youth of the day is of interest.

Sentinel DG6T three-way tipper No 7711, Registration No KP 4476, built *circa* 1929 and sold to Will & Packham Ltd of Sittingbourne, Kent.

Sentinel DG6 waggon No 8117, Registration No UX 5849, built 1929. The records show that she was new to W.E.C. Clark of London. Perhaps they were the selling agents or the parent company as this is a works photograph and shows her when new in Smith Bros livery. She was last licenced in December 1932, a very short life!

Sentinel DG6 waggon No 7422, Registration No RR 9407, built 1928 and sold to Cafferata & Co Ltd of Newark-upon-Trent.